Enspired
UNDER HIS WINGS

KIMBERLY MCALLISTER

authorHOUSE®

AuthorHouse™
1663 Liberty Drive
Bloomington, IN 47403
www.authorhouse.com
Phone: 1 (800) 839-8640

Published by AuthorHouse 02/15/2016

ISBN: 978-1-5049-7459-2 (sc)
ISBN: 978-1-5049-7458-5 (e)

Library of Congress Control Number: 2016900998

Print information available on the last page.

Dedication

This book is dedicated to my mom.
Who has always been an inspiration in my life.
You are truly a mother of strength, wisdom, and faith.
You never tell me what I want to hear. But you
always tell me what I need to hear. And for
that I am truly thankful.
Thank you for loving me with the Love of Christ.
I love you.

A Moment Of Reflection

These God-inspired poems were given to
me from God to heal the soul,
and bring deliverance to the weary spirit.
It wasn't until I surrendered
my heart to God that i realized that He
was using my life experiences
as footprints for those who would go
through the same things that I've
been through. He allowed me to go through
trials and tribulations to
be a blessing to others through poetic
writing. This book was written
to send healing to those who struggle with fear, insecurity, low-self
esteem, depression, oppression, rejection,
and negativity. It's my desire
to know that through these beautiful collective poems, someone is
being delivered, and healed from past and
present wounds. I Pray that
you will enjoy them as much as I do.. God Bless....

Acknowledgements

I first would like to acknowledge my Lord and Savior Jesus Christ; who continually brings me through all my trials and tribulations. If it had not been for God showing me what real love is, I would not be here today. I secondly would like to acknowledge my mother who has always been there for me. Thank you for being a great support in all my endeavors. For always telling me what I needed to hear and not what I wanted to hear (never sugar coating the truth). I say from the depths of my heart, I LOVE YOU!

Thirdly I acknowledge my husband, who has been my friend, and support. You've always been there when I was sick and discouraged; I thank you for honoring our vows before God and loving me unconditionally. Acknowledgments also go to my sister, brothers, children, grandchildren, and also to my mentor and servant of the Most High God, Norris Porter, who has always encouraged me to pursue the things of God.

Proverbs 18:17-

Iron sharpeneth iron; so a man sharpeneth the countenance of his friend.

A friendship that will last

I'm so glad that we met.
My heart can't contain.
Forever through life.
Our friendship will remain.
My prayer partner in a time of need.
With words of inspiration, in me, you have planted a seed.
God has given me someone so dear, so true.
No one else can ever take the place of you.
This is a friendship that will last.

Psalm 51:7-10

7 Purge me with hyssop, and I shall be clean: wash me, and I shall be whiter than snow. 8 Make me to hear joy and gladness; that the bones which thou hast broken may rejoice. 9 Hide thy face from my sins, and blot out all mine iniquities. 10 Create in me a clean heart, O God; and renew a right spirit within me.

An Open Vessel For The Lord

Lord take this vessel of mine
Cleanse me, clean me out
Make me over
I have filled it with so much filth
Take out of me all that does not please you
It is a stench in your nostrils
Let the aroma of my sincere heart
Be like frankincense in your presence
I desire to be used by you
Show me what you want me to do
Teach me oh God
For I am a vessel
An open vessel for you Lord

Ecclesiastes 2:11

Yet when I surveyed all that my hands had done and what I had toiled to achieve, everything was meaningless, a chasing after the wind; nothing was gained under the sun.

Chasing The Wind

I was out there in the world trying to cover my shame.
I thought I was hiding from reality, it was all a game.
Chasing the wind, looking for satisfaction.
Giving my flesh what it wanted, my flesh craved for more action.
My life was one big mess, it was hard at times, I must confess.
Chasing the wind is all that I use to do.
Ohhh until that wonderful day that I was introduced to you.
You opened up my heart and stored in me your precious love.
Nothing in this world can compare to you,
my heavenly Father from above.
I no longer chase the wind. I chase only after you.
You have showed your love to me.
Your love Lord is faithful and true.

Luke 15:20

"And he arose and came back to his father. But when he was still a great way off, his father saw him and had compassion, and ran and fell on his neck and kissed him."

Come Home To The Father's House

Come home to the Father's House
Where peace will be your friend
Come home to the Father's House
Where joy will hold your hand
Come home to the Father's House
He's waiting with His heart wide open
Come home to the Father's House
He gave us Jesus as a sacrificial token
Come home to the Father's house
Where there is an overflow of love
Come home to the Father's House
You're the one he's thinking of
Come Home

Jeremiah 1:5

Before I formed thee in the belly I knew thee; and before thou camest forth out of the womb I sanctified thee, [and] I ordained thee a prophet unto the nations.

Did you know

Did you know
That He cares for you
Did you know
He's there when you're going through
Did you know
That He holds you near
Did you know
That He saves all your tears
Did you know
His Son died for you
Did you know
His word is true
Did you know
You are the apple of His eye
Did you know
Did you know

Hebrew 12:2

Looking unto Jesus the author and finisher of our faith; who for the joy that was set before him endured the cross, despising the shame, and is set down at the right hand of the throne of God.

I Keep Seeing Jesus

Laying here in tears, I keep seeing Jesus.
As each tear hits my pillow, I see them hitting Jesus.
As this world speaks words of hate to me, I
see them spitting on my sweet Jesus.
Betrayals all around me, but I keep seeing Jesus.
The pressures of the world are trying to weigh me down.
But I keep seeing Jesus baring the cross.
When my feet hit the floor in the morning and i arise.
I see Jesus being raised on the cross.
With the words of victory on my lips.
I see Jesus, snatching the keys from the enemy.
So each day in my life, I will snatch the
keys from the enemy because
I keep seeing Jesus.

2 Corinthians 4:13

We having the same spirit of faith, according as it is written, I believed, and therefore have I spoken.

I Speak

I speak to the mountains that rise high in my life.
Mountains of poverty, mountains of fear, and mountains of strife.
I speak to the things that once lived, now have died.
I speak to the lame, take up your bed and rise.
I speak to the sick and say be healed.
I speak to the empty jars, and I say be filled.
I speak a word in due season.
I speak protection at night.
And I speak words.
That is pleasing.
I speak.

John 7:38

He that believeth on me, as the scripture hath said, out of his belly shall flow rivers of living water

Let It Flow

There's a song in my heart that the angels can't comprehend.
There's praise in my spirit, that when I'm
down, only praise can mend.
Let it flow, Let it flow.
There's a deep, deep fountain that only God can fill.
There's a river that runs deep inside of me, Lord,
that in your presence, I desire to just stand still.
Let it flow, Let it flow.
There's a mountain that stands so strong, unmovable.
But with you on my side, I can speak to that
mountain, and the mountain must go.
Let it flow, Let it flow
My heart sings
Let it flow, Let it flow

Roman 12:2

And be not conformed to this world: but be ye transformed by the renewing of your mind, that ye may prove what is that good, and acceptable, and perfect, will of God.

Lost In Me

I look around at beauty that is not of me.
Straight hair, light-skin.
Lost in me.
My kinky curls, are not acceptable in their sight.
Blonde hair, thin lips.
Lost in me all day and all night.
The run way is not made for a girl like me.
Thin waste, thin thighs.
Lost in me.
One day I'm going to find me.
Cause I see a little window inside of me.
And I'm breaking through the shadow,
Of insecurity.
At the end I will no longer be,
Lost in me.

Mark 11:24

Therefore I say unto you, What things soever ye desire, when ye pray, believe that ye receive them, and ye shall have them.

Receive

I've held my hands out all day for you to receive.
I've heard all of your prayers and know all your needs.
Receive.
Secret prayers, I've made my first priority.
And all I've ever wanted you to do was just believe
Receive.
My love for you out weighs your faults.
Your ways are not my ways and your
thoughts are not my thoughts.
Receive.
I hear your prayers, even when you're on your knees
And all I am saying to you is just
Receive.

Acts 3:19

Repent ye therefore, and be converted, that your sins may be blotted out, when the times of refreshing shall come from the presence of the Lord

Talking To The Church

I'm talking to the church, cause I seen a lot going down.
From the pulpit, to the elders, to the choir
dressed in their crisp white gown.
Your in God's temple, yes with your
hands stretched towards the skies.
Your mouth says you love him, but your heart speaks terrible lies.
Wolves in sheep clothing, undetected by others.
But the Holy Ghost will expose you,
and even the seasoned mothers.
You keep yourselves busy with every detail of the sanctuary.
While your house is kept undone, leaving your family to tarry.
I'm talking to the church, cause I can't take this no more.
You live off the fat of the land by stealing offerings from the poor.
Your prayers have become witchcraft, a snare to your very soul.
Repent, Repent before it's to late, those
worldy things, I beg of you, let go.
Your deeds are being recorded, the angels of God see all.
The lust of the eyes, lust of the flesh and the pride
of life will make the strongest man fall
You see I'm talking to the Church, cause
God loves you in spite of your sin.
Repent, and be delivered so His Holy Spirit can dwell within.

Jeremiah 30:17

For I will restore health unto thee, and I will heal thee of thy wounds, saith the LORD; because they called thee an Outcast, saying, This is Zion, whom no man seeketh after.

The Pieces Of My Life

I allowed this thing to go on too long.
And I'm tired of singing the lyrics to your old song.
I have to find my own way, and stand on my own.
I can see the path that's leading to my own home.
Struggled for so many years with insecurity.
Cause I let your lies get the best of me.
The pieces of my life.
Never had the time to get over you.
Raising your kids, work and night school.
What a fool I've been for believing that you could change.
Two strangers in our bed and I hear you calling her name.
The pieces of my life.
So glad I turned this page in my life.
Trying to be a mother and a dedicated wife.
You took the best of me, cause you thought
without you, there is no me.
But I'm still standing, stronger than ever as you can see.
Better and wiser without you, yes I'm free.
The pieces of my life.
As I go on this journey called life.
I'm picking up the pieces of my life.
I'm holding on to what's mine.
In the hands of God, I'll be fine.
Oh yea the pieces of my life.

Deuteronomy 6:5

And thou shalt love the LORD thy God with all thine heart, and with all thy soul, and with all thy mights.

What You Are To Me

A comforter is what you are to me.
Trustworthy and kind to all you see.
You are my hero, my dear friend in my time of need.
You encourage me to be the best that I can be.
You understand my heart, my hurt, my pain.
In my time with you, there is so much that I gain.
My Husband, My Friend, My Healer
That is what you are to me

John 14:6

Jesus saith unto him, I am the way, the truth, and the life: no man cometh unto the Father, but by me.

I Am

I will wipe your tears
I Am your comforter
I will heal your land
I Am your healer
I will bring freedom to your soul
I Am your redeemer
I will give you joy
I Am your peace
I will, what I will to do
Cause I Am all that I Am
For I Am the
Great I Am

<u>Psalm 50:15</u>

"Call upon Me in the day of trouble; I shall rescue you, and you will honor Me."

I Can Call On The Lord

Anytime of the day, I can call on the Lord
When he seems far away, I can call on the Lord
When all hope seems to be gone, I can call on the Lord
When my body is rocking in pain, I can call on the Lord
Whether I have friends or friends not, I can call on the Lord
At times when I don't do right, I can call on the Lord
When my mind is restless, can't sleep at
night, I can call on the Lord
I can call on the Lord for anything I need
Even with faith the size of a mustard seed

Psalm 103:1

Bless the Lord O my soul: and all that is within me, bless his holy name.

Oh Come Bless The King

Oh come all and bless the King
His faithfulness endures forever
Let us all sing
Oh come all who serve the King
For His deliverance endures forever
Let us all sing
Oh come all and touch the Kings Healing garment
His Healing power endures forever
Let us all sing
Ohh come all and bless
The King

Acts 17:27

That they should seek the Lord, if haply they might feel after him, and find him.

Search And Find Me

You can look for me in the heavens
You can look for me in the sea
You can look beyond the horizons
Search with all your heart if needed be
You can search the world all over
And search the waters deep
Search and you will find me
In your inner peace

Psalm 34:1

I will bless the LORD at all times: his praise shall continually be in my mouth.

You Can Call On The Lord

Who is your Provider
In a time of need
Who is your Deliverer
When deliverance need be
Who is your Healer
When the pain has you down
Who is your Redeemer
When you're feeling bound
Who is your Father
When you've been disowned
Who is your Friend
When you're feeling all alone
Who is your Warrior
Whose words is sharper than a sword
Who can you call on
You can call on the Lord

Psalm 127:3

Lo, children are an heritage of the Lord: and the fruit of the womb is his reward.

A Mother And Daughters Love

I have wiped the tears from your eyes
Now you wipe my tears
I have combed your hair with love
Now, you gently comb my hair, with love
And as I have held your hands, so many times
Now you hold my hands, to let me know you are still there
When you were young, I watched over you
like a hen watches over her eggs
And in return you watch over me, making
sure that I am given the best care
The same worries that I once had about you, you have about me
It lets me know that I have done well by you.
And now you are doing well by me.

Proverbs 31:10

Who can find a virtuous woman

A Woman Of Confidence

A woman of assurance is what they call her. Her assurance comes from God. She wears a robe of confidence in everything she does. Blessed is what people call her. Anointed is what she is. She is praised in everything she does, because God is with her. Admired by men and women, because her walk is a walk of godliness, and not of the world. As she walks by, she leaves an aroma of myrrh and frankincense in the air. Blessed will be her husband, blessed will be her children, and blessed will be her grandchildren. She's in preparation when a trial comes, always depending on God, and no one else. She's prayed up to the fullest. Her words are delicately spoken, ready to heal the broken hearted, ready to shame the wicked with loving words. Wrath is uncomfortable around her. Peace purges her continually. Her smile comforts her surroundings. A woman of assurance is what she is, and blessed she is in all her ways.

Jeremiah 29:11

*For I know the thoughts that I think toward you, saith the L*ORD, *thoughts of peace, and not of evil, to give you an expected end.*

Back to me

I been away from myself for so long.
Longing and crying to come home.
Letting trials and circumstances get me down.
All alone, even though everyone's around.
Heard a voice say come back to yourself.
So I'll take wings like an angel and leave the rest for everyone else.
Many times looking in the mirror trying to find a piece of me.
Trying to get nearer and back to me.
Back to me, back to me, oh yea back to me.
I said I'm tired of trying to be this perfect package.
Gotta hold my head up, be strong, instead of
feeding into negativity and reacting.
Just let me be myself, I don't want to be like anyone else.
God made me different for a reason.
I declare I'm coming back to me in this season.
I'm coming back to myself, no second thoughts,
putting my troubles on the shelf.
Whether you agree or disagree.
I'm coming back to me.
Cause I long to be free and back to me.

2 Corinthians 6:14

Be ye not unequally yoked together with unbelievers: for what fellowship hath righteousness with unrighteousness? and what communion hath light with darkness?

Bitter But Sweet

It took me a long time to get to this place in my life.
To finally come to grips with the fact
that I'm no longer your wife.
You signed the papers and I did too, thought
I could hold on to your love.
What was I thinking; my friends say that I'm a fool.
Sad to know that our bitter, sweet
memories are a thing of the pass.
A part of me was hoping and praying
that this marriage would last.
Bitter but sweet.
Even though we said goodbye in the courtroom.
My heart has no place for friendship, but
I'm hoping it will real soon.
Can't believe I let your insecurities tear me down.
Playing games with my head, and holding me bound.
Many times I had to cry myself to sleep.
And many times I couldn't laugh, think and couldn't eat.
Bitter but sweet.
I spent many days asking God to make it better.
Praying he would make it right, and you and I would be together.
It took me a long time to realize.
A long time to become strong and wipe my teary eyes.
Each day is like a breaking of a new life.
No more beatings, no more cheating, and no more strife.
Bitter but sweet.

Esther 4:14

For if thou altogether holdest thy peace at this time, then shall there enlargement and deliverance arise to the Jews from another place; but thou and thy father's house shall be destroyed: and who knoweth whether thou art come to the kingdom for such a time as this?

For Such A Time Like This

Your prayers are not prayers that are just a mist
They have been instilled inside your heart
For such a time like this
The testing of your faith has shined through like pure gold
And the desires of your heart are about to unfold
The time has been set, the angles are waiting
Step into your destiny, without debating
It is not Gods will for you to go without
He gave you that spirit of Joshua, to march around
the walls and claim victory with a shout
His strength inside of you
Gives you the ability to do what he has called you to do
Your hands are anointed and your voice too
His holy spirit will guide you as you're going through
No, your prayers are not prayers that are just a mist
You have been called for such a time like this

Ephesians 4:6 ~

One God and Father of all, who [is] above all, and through all, and in you all.

God The Father, My Strength

Like the strength of a slave I continue to
take the whips on my back.
Raising my head every now and then to breathe.
Only to have my head pushed back down into the ground.
But with every breath, I strive for the goal of winning in Christ.
Is this the path that God laid out for me?
Does he know something that I don't know?
He said his thoughts are higher than mine.
If he can only give me an idea of what
he's trying to work out in me.
Give me a glimpse of what I will become.
Then maybe I can hold on a little longer.
Isn't it great to know that God doesn't
see us the way we see ourselves.
You see that's what keeps me going.
Knowing that my Father in heaven knows
that there is more to me than just me.
And that gives me strength.

1 John 3:15

Whosoever hateth his brother is a murderer: and ye know that no murderer hath eternal life abiding in him.

I Was Killing You Softly (1 john 3:15)

Sister, I repent of my sins. Please Forgive me. Repent of what you ask? I've been killing you softly. I've been smiling in your face, while tearing your character down behind your back. When you came to me for prayer, I turned your situation, into a teatime conversation. When you offered to volunteer I turned you away without a second thought. The times you needed to talk, I only listened so I could have something to talk about later. You see I had a reputation to uphold. I couldn't be seen tending to someone who was not on my level, at least that's what they would always say. I've killed you, before anyone even met you. I created for them a book of your life. Remember you mentioned about how you would get funny looks? I repent, I've looked upon you like you were nothing. Killing you softly. . ... bringing you to the lowest, while I put on a form of godliness, exalting myself in front of others. With my white crisp dress and matching hat, I would swing into the house of God, looking like I have it all together. Oh what I appeared to be. If they only knew the thoughts of my mind. God commands me to love thy neighbor. But you see, I couldn't do that, I was too into myself. My friends, my car, my job, and what others would think, got the best of me. I was worried about being kicked out of their clique. Too afraid of what they would say if i became your friend. But you see, there's a light opening up in me, and my soul is not at ease. I ask for your forgiveness and maybe you will find it in your heart to pray for me. I'm a sister in need of prayer, and maybe just maybe your prayer will reach the ear of God. Forgive me for killing you softly.

Deuteronomy 28:2

All these blessings will come upon you and overtake you if you obey the Lord your God.

I'm Blessed

As I look over my life- I'm blessed
As I sit in my room- I'm not alone
As I speak to the stranger on the street —I'm filled with joy
As I speak to my heart- I'm comforted
As I walk along the seashore- I'm in your presence God
As I sit with my friends- I'm in good company
As I look upon my children's eyes, I see many nations
As I enter you're sanctuary- my heart begins to worship you
As the enemy tries to tell me lies- I'm drawn
even closer to my blessings, yes I'm blessed
The lady that I am- she tells me I'm so blessed
Even when they look down on me, it never gets
the best of me cause- I'm just too blessed
As I confess my healing- I'm blessed
As I look outside my window i see the blessings of
God, they're falling, and falling into the arms
of those who will receive him- and they are truly blessed

<u>*Psalm 31:15*</u>

My times are in Your hand; Deliver me from the hand of my enemies and from those who persecute me.

Just a season

At times life becomes difficult and unsure.
Worries and anxiety seem to take their position upon our lives.
And we just can't find our way out.
We look but can't find.
We cry but the problem increases more.
But one thing is for sure.
This is just a season.
And seasons in our lives must change.
As winter becomes spring.
And summer becomes fall.
They all have one thing in common, change.
The same is with your life.
It must change, because nothing stays the same
And when it does, your life is refreshed, restored and renewed.
And it seems as if nothing has happened.
So with knowing this lets remain still and
listen to the lesson that is being taught
Enjoy our loved ones and examine the
beauty of life and the giver of life.
Let's focus on what's more important in our lives.
Let's remember that this is a test, a season,
and in due time it must change.

To the suffering; I say to you
Be still and know that God is in control.

Psalm 147:3

He heals the brokenhearted and binds up their wounds.

Sister can we talk

Hello sister can I talk to you for a minute. Yes you. You see we have a lot in common. From your dark-shaded glasses to your long sleeve shirt. I've been watching you, not to get into your business but just to acknowledge how good the lord has been to me. You see I can relate to you.

Sister can we talk?

Your eyes tell many stories, and your tears show deep, deep pain. I can understand how you confuse him loving you with his words and him loving you with his fist. Some days you probably think that he doesn't love you unless he hits you. It's a different language isn't it?

Sister can we talk?

It seems like the slaps say I miss you and the punches say I love you. Don't be deceived, that's not love. Love doesn't cause you to hide your beautiful face behind dark shades. Love doesn't take away the very precious thing that God gave you, your self-esteem. Love doesn't take away the love you once had for yourself.

Sister can we talk?

You see I've been there and done that. Me and every other woman on the face of this earth. How many live to tell the story? Only God knows. Blessed are the ones who survive. Peace, to the ones who never got a chance to tell their story or kiss their mother, father, sister, brother or child goodbye.

Sister can we talk?

*Your worried about him? Don't worry about him. When he's
finished with you, he'll do the same to another. Survival and
control is his game, let it be yours. What is a man who belittles
another just to make himself feel superior? You've got it. Who
helped me? My brother, his name is Jesus. Who made sure that
he wouldn't touch me again? My father, God in heaven. So sister
take my hand and let me guide you to the goodness of God
Will you come? You will. Bless you sister
Let's talk*

1 Samuel 3:10

*And the LORD came, and stood, and called as at other times,
Samuel, Samuel. Then Samuel answered, Speak; for thy servant
heareth.*

Speak Lord

Speak Lord
To the one who has lost their way
Speak Lord
To the one who is speechless, not knowing what to think or say
Speak Lord
To your child who feels all alone
Speak Lord
To the unknown
Speak Lord
To the heart that desires to know you
Speak Lord
To the one who is going through
Speak Lord
So that the sun will shine again
Speak Lord
To the one who needs a praying friend
Speak Lord
And let your breath fill the air with everlasting life
Speak Lord
Remove confusion, heartache, and strife
Speak Lord

Joshua 24:15

And if it seem evil unto you to serve the Lord, choose you this day whom ye will serve;

The choice is yours

You have a choice to live
A choice to die
A choice to laugh
And a choice to cry
A choice to curse
And a choice to bless
A choice to do things halfway
And a choice to give your best
A choice to turn away those in need
And a choice to sow in their life, a seed
A choice to live in affliction, fear and infirmity
And a choice to be healed, in faith,
and prosperity
A choice to hate
And a choice to love
A choice to go to hell
And a choice to live heavenly above
but just remember one thing
The Choice Is Yours

Genesis 1:26

And God said, Let us make man in our image, after our likeness

The color of your skin it doesn't matter

People making a big deal about the color of your skin
I'm not concerned about that
I'm more interested in the person within
The same Lord that heals the white, heals the black
Different colors but their seeds still never lack
The same color blood flows through you and I
We're both young one moment, then old, and then we die
So it doesn't matter what color the Lord may be
What does matter is that he set me free
Senseless talk about Jesus was a black
man, Jesus was a white man
Can you change the color of his words?
I'll like to see if you can
His words show no partiality
He loves you and he loves me
Please don't put his name to shame
Love your fellow brother and sister in Jesus name

Psalm 34:19

Many are the afflictions of the righteous: but the LORD delivereth him out of them all.

When Trouble Comes

Backtracking into my mind, sadness tries to overtake me.
The devil and his host of demons try to break me.
Thinking about the let downs, the torment and pain.
But then I bow my head in prayer and call on Jesus name.
I look on the inner beauty, the light that shines within.
The light that brought me out of darkness,
and washed me of my sin.
I hear his voice, he tells me to stand.
In praise and glory to him, I began to wave my hand.
When trouble comes, I am not moved, I bow
my head, your words they soothe.
When trouble comes, your name is close to mind.
I pray to you and peace I find.
When trouble comes, I see your salvation.
Your power and might.
Upon all creation.

Psalm 46:1-2

God is our refuge and strength, A very present help in trouble.

You helped me lord

You helped me Lord, wipe away my tears, I've been crying
From the abuse for so many years. Blow after
blow, I would pray in my heart,
That the beatings would stop, and the love
would start. Being told constantly that i
was nothing. But you came in, molded me, and
made me something. Empty and lonely
is what I felt at times, longing to have a
peace that would only be mine.
Caught up in darkness I heard your voice call
out to me. You heard and helped me
Lord, yes you heard my plead. I'm so
grateful for having you in my life.
In my house now dwells peace, and no longer lives strife.

Psalm 26:3

He restoreth my soul: he leadeth me in the paths of righteousness for his name's sake

Footnotes

I've been walking through this life for some time
With only pleasure on my mind
Never thought about whose feelings I would hurt
Wasted my time on relationships that never worked
Simple things never fulfilled my inward parts
Peaceful things I would never let come into my heart
Is my life a piece of paper, blank or maybe plain
People who think they know me, but they
don't even know my name
What's my purpose I keep hearing people say
Is my life a wasted walk day by day
I think I'll leave little footnotes in the rain
So the generations to come won't have to
suffer from some of my pain
I'll leave footnotes of strength as I go by
Strength with wings to make you stronger, and to make you fly
I think I'll leave footnotes in the rain
So the generations to come won't have to suffer from my pain
I'll leave footnotes of wisdom for them to pick up too
So they won't have to figure out what they should say or do
Yea, I've been walking through this life for some time
With only pleasure on my mind
Never thought now that I could have a life, fresh, anew
Now I have someone that I can tell my problems to
All those years of disappointments, sickness, and abuse too
I realized that I had to endure, so I could
leave footnotes of wisdom just for you
So I'll keep leaving footnotes through my life
So you won't have to endure all of the worlds' confusion and strife
I hope my footnotes will fit your feet just right
If they fit you, they will lead you to your destiny in Jesus Christ
Oh yes, I'll keep leaving footnotes in the rain
So the next generation won't have to suffer from my pain

Philippians 4:19

But my God shall supply all your need according to his riches in glory by Christ Jesus

God Did It Again

When I was sinking deep in sin
God came in, grabbed my hands
And pulled me in
God did it again
When I was hungry, No money to buy food
A man put a bag of groceries on my steps
I cried Lord, this can only be you
God did it again
My bills were due, lights soon to be cut off
I turned off the t.v., fell to my knees
It was God's face I sought
God did it again
Doctors gave up on me
Said there was nothing they could do
Scripture says by His stripes I'm healed
Now my body is healed, and made new
God did it again

1 Peter 2:9

But ye are a chosen generation, a royal priesthood, an holy nation, a peculiar people

I Know Who God Has Created Me To Be

It doesn't matter what the enemy says to me
And it doesn't matter what you see in me
I know who God has created me to be
Not to sound disrespectful like I'm all that
I'm just confident in my skin
I'm young, gifted and black
So it doesn't matter what the enemy says to me
And it doesn't matter what you see in me
I know who God has created me to be
You see I put my dress on, one leg at a time
And I declare my healing, my healing I know is mine
My suffering and my pain
Doesn't discredit Jesus as my Savior
Cause my healing is in His Blood Stain
I still stand on His word, I know who He has created me to be
It doesn't matter what the enemy says to me

2 Corinthians 5:17

Therefore if any man be in Christ, he is a new creature: old things are passed away; behold, all things are become new

I Was, I Am

I was the face of Rebellion
I was the face of Hate
I was the face of Insecurity
I was the face of Prejudice
I was the face of Rape
You may ask yourself, what are you now?
I am the face of Obedience
I am the face of Love
I am the face of Confidence
I am the face of Unity
I am the face of Wholeness
I am Woman, Born again of God

Psalm 24:9

*Lift up your heads, O ye gates; even lift them up, ye everlasting
doors; and the King of glory shall come in*

Lifter Of My Soul

You're the lifter of my soul
You're my heartbeat when I wanna let go
You're my healer in times of distress
You're my peace when I'm going through my test
You're my protector when fear tries to enter in
You're the victory in me because you died for my sin
My lifter you are over my enemies
You are my lifter of my soul
By your power you have parted the deep red sea
You are the lifter, you are the lifter, and you are the lifter
The lifter of my soul

Philippians 4:8

Finally, brethren, whatsoever things are true, whatsoever things are honest, whatsoever things are just, whatsoever things are pure, whatsoever things are lovely, whatsoever things are of good report; if there be any virtue, and if there be any praise, think on these things.

Think On These Things

When I think on your salvation
And how you saved me
My soul rejoices in you
Because you and only you have made me free
When I think on your love and kindness
Thanksgiving fills my heart
Tears of joy over take me
Because you loved me right from the start
When I think on how you called me
Words cannot explain
You've healed my open wounds, and took away my pain
When I think on the great sacrifice
Your son Jesus Christ
Who died for all to be saved
He has paid the ultimate price

John 8:36

If the Son therefore shall make you free, ye shall be free indeed.

Who The Son Sets Free, Is Free Indeed

God said it in his word
Who the Son sets free
Is free, free, free indeed
He's not a God that He would lie
So, leave the bondage behind
Who the Son sets free
Is free indeed
Free from the pain
Free from the sin
Free from the guilt you carry within
Just take Him at His word
Leave the bondage behind
Who the Son sets free is free indeed
Free from the pain
Free from the sin
Free from the guilt you carry with
Who the Son sets free is free indeed

Luke 2:11

For unto you is born this day in the city of David a Savior which is Christ the Lord.

Beautiful Savior

Beautiful Savior how wonderful you are
One can't help but to cry before your presence
He without sin, bore our sin, to bring us into his glory
My heart awaits with anxiousness, to know your will for my life
I wait in expectancy, to hear from you O' Lord
For I understand not your ways, but I
waiver not in my trust in you
Because I know your thoughts and ways are best for me,
So I put all my confidence in you
My Beautiful Savior
how excellent you are
The oceans moves at your commands
The birds fly high in praise of your beauty
The moon acknowledges your presence
The mountains exalt you in the highest praise
Beautiful Savior
Let me behold all of you
Let me remain in you
So that all the days of my life
Can be counted as blessed by God
My Beautiful savior

Ecclesiastes 3:1

To every thing there is a season, and a time to every purpose under the heaven:

Seasons

There are seasons when we will laugh
Seasons when we will cry
Seasons when we will live
Seasons when our loved ones will die

Seasons when our health is strong
Seasons when nothing can go wrong
Seasons when we have friends
Seasons when our friendships must end

Seasons when we are content with what we own
Seasons when we must walk alone
Seasons when we are loved by many
Seasons when true love is not plenty

Seasons when we grow into maturity
Seasons when we realize the harsh truths of reality
Seasons when we are vibrant and young
Seasons when we sang from our heart old hymn songs
In all these things are seasons and they will change

Psalm 106:1

Praise ye the Lord. O give thanks unto the Lord;
for he is good: for his mercy endureth for ever.

I Shall Praise Thee Oh Lord

I Shall praise thee oh lord

I shall praise thee oh lord
My strength in a time of need

I shall praise thee oh lord
your word you give to me

I shall praise thee oh lord
morning, noon, and night

I shall praise thee oh lord
with all my heart, soul, and might

Amen, and Amen

Psalm 34:19

Many are the afflictions of the righteous: but the LORD delivereth him out of them all.

Dear Lord...

My troubles are nothing

Compared to what you have in store for me, oh God.

I rejoice in them, I rejoice in my suffering, for they are many.

And while I rejoice, my eyes are in watch of my enemies.

They flee at your rebuke, ooh God.

like the snake that ate up pharaoh's snakes,

you eat up all that surround me.

So why should I be troubled?

For you are the God of Abraham, Isaac, and Jacob.

And I've seen your mighty hands at work

in the lives of those who call you, Abba Father.

Praise thee the lord, for you are good for the soul

Philippians 1:10

That ye may approve things that are excellent; that ye may be sincere and without offence till the day of Christ;

Prayer Of Sincerity

When the storms come and I feel overtaken.
I remember your words, and I
am not forsaken. Always will I rejoice in
your name, my Lord, my Savior, I
will always proclaim. My Lord help me to
learn how to live with little or none.
So the tricks of the enemy I can overcome.
Perfection is what you desire. So
Fill me with your Holy Ghost, set my soul on fire.

1 Corinthians 13:11

When I was a child, I spake as a child, I understood as a child, I thought as a child: but when I became a man, I put away childish things.

The Child In Me

If you take a glimpse into my eyes
You'll find a little child inside
A child whose innocence was taken away
A child who has been whipped with words
A child whose dark caramel skin is not acceptable by many
A child who had to fight for her freedom
A child who has overcome obstacles
Because she was given them at such a young age
A child who was given independence as a gift from God
A child who embraces her beauty from within
A child who learned confidence in the mist of her diversities
Yes take a glimpse into my eyes
And see the child
Who has become a woman

2 Samuel 22:50

Therefore I will give thanks unto thee, O LORD, among the heathen, and I will sing praises unto thy name.

Shall I Praise Him

Shall I Praise Him
Praise Him
He woke me up this morning
Praise Him
He gave me a new life
Praise Him
He set me free
Praise Him
He guides my footsteps
Praise Him
He hold me in the midnight hour
Praise Him
He gives me unconditional love
Praise Him
He keeps me when I think I can't be kept
Praise Him
so I ask myself
Shall I Praise Him

1 Thessalonians 5:18

In every thing give thanks for this is the will of God in Christ Jesus concerning you.

Giving Thanks From The Heart

Giving thanks from the heart
You've done so many things for me; I don't know where to start.
Should I start when you shaped me in my mother's womb?
Or when you sent Jesus to die for our sins,
then later him being raised from
His tomb. There are so many things to thank
you for, where should I begin?
You loved me when I was a sinner in the
world, and even promised to love
me now and even til the end. Thank you
for my mother who loves me
Unconditional. Thank you for my children,
their love for me I enfold.
Thank you for the many times you healed
me, when I wasn't well, your
Healing hands I would always see. When
I felt like I couldn't go on. You
commanded your angels to minister to me,
in My heart giving me a new
song. So Father as we sit together, enjoying
each others company. Let's
give thanks to the giver of life, without
him this Day would not be.

Amen

Ephesians 6:13

Wherefore take unto you the whole armour of God, that ye may be able to withstand in the evil day, and having done all, to stand.

Will you stand anyhow?

Here's a question
Will you stand when times are hard?
When the promotion seems so far.
Will you stand when your back is against the wall?
Will you stand when your family turns
against you, yes Will you stand tall?
When the rent is do will you stand?
Even though the money is not in your hand.
Seeing that your children are going without.
Anxiety and anger makes you want to shout.
Will you stand when the pressure tries to overtake you.
when your feeling like God has forsaken you, will you stand?
Stand anyhow family or not.
When they depart God will take up their spot
Stand anyhow with money or no money at all.
The love of money makes greedy people fall.
I understand the anger you want to release.
Shout out to God to take the burden and give you peace.
So the questions remains the same.
Will you stand?

Matthew 21:16

And said unto him, Hearest thou what these say? And Jesus saith unto them, Yea; have ye never read, Out of the mouth of babes and sucklings thou hast perfected praise?

Perfect Praise

In my darkest hour when I thought
I was all alone
Soft-spoken words, to my master on
His throne
It has gotten me
through those tough days
I will never leave you nor forsake you,
The Lord would say
You've cleansed my heart, and made
me whole
To you I give thanks, to
you I owe
You're always Guiding me on
my way
Through my trials and through those
rough days
I have over come; victory has been placed
in my hands
To you I give thanks, for
you I stand
Because you've cleansed my heart, and made
me whole
To you I give thanks, to
you I owe

Luke 8:24

They came to Jesus and woke Him up, saying, "Master, Master, we are perishing!" And He got up and rebuked the wind and the surging waves, and they stopped, and it became calm.

Even Though The Storm Is Over Now

Even though
the storm is over now
Even though my
mind is at peace, it's sound
I will bless
your holy name
Because my
life is not the same

You've showered
me with so much grace and love
There's no
other God that I think of
I can't
believe it's true, that I've found someone like you

So even though
I close my eyes at night
I pray to you
to keep me Lord, keep me right
I will bless
your holy name
Because my life
is not the same

Even though my
friends have walked away
Even at times I
don't know what to say
I will bless
your holy name
Because my life
is not the same

Even though the
storm is over now
Even though my
mind is at peace, it's sound
I will bless
your holy name
Because my life
is not the same

Printed in the United States
By Bookmasters